SCIENCE
AROUND
THE
HOUSE

Also by Robert Gardner

Kitchen Chemistry
    Science Experiments to Do at Home

Water
    The Life-Sustaining Resource

The Whale Watchers' Guide

SCIENCE AROUND THE HOUSE

ROBERT GARDNER

Illustrated by Frank Cecala

JULIAN MESSNER · NEW YORK

Published by Julian Messner,
A Division of Simon & Schuster, Inc.
Simon & Schuster Building
Rockefeller Center
1230 Avenue of the Americas
New York, New York 10020

JULIAN MESSNER and colophon are
trademarks of Simon & Schuster, Inc.

Manufactured in the United States of America

Library ed. 10 9 8 7 6 5 4

Paper ed. 10 9 8 7 6 5 4 3 2

Library of Congress Cataloging-in-Publication Data

Gardner, Robert, 1929—
   Science around the house.

   Includes index.
   Summary: Instructions for science experiments to do
at home in such areas as gravity, velocity, and weights.

   1. Science—Experiments—Juvenile literature.
2. Physics—Experiments—Juvenile literature.
3. Scientific recreations—Juvenile literature.
[1. Science—Experiments. 2. Physics—Experiments.
3. Experiments] I. Title.
Q164.G34   1985   507.8   85-8873
ISBN: 0-671-54663-5 (Library ed.)
ISBN: 0-671-68139-7 (Paper ed.)

CONTENTS

SCIENCE AROUND THE HOUSE

PREFACE

Your home, in addition to being a place to eat, sleep, and live, is a good environment in which to carry out science experiments. Your kitchen has hot and cold water for experiments that require it. There is a refrigerator where you can prepare ice or cool substances to very low temperatures. The stove allows you to heat or dry a wide variety of materials.

Your bathroom and kitchen together provide many useful chemicals that can be used in experiments, and, of course, your bathtub is an excellent place to immerse large objects including your own body if you want to know how much space you take up.

A stairwell is an excellent place to find out about falling objects. Your basement probably contains a number of tools useful in building apparatus for experiments and for measuring results. Even the walls, ceilings, and floors of your house, as you will see, can help you learn more about science.

Of course, other members of your family are not going to be very happy if they stumble over your apparatus as they walk about the house. Your parents and siblings will be more tolerant of your experiments and more eager to listen to your accounts of them if you don't interfere with their lives. So clean up after you finish each session. Thoughtful scientists do not let their work interfere with the activities of others. If your experiment must be conducted over a long period of time, try to set it up in a place that is out of the way of other people.

Do all your experiments with care, especially those in which you use a stove, matches, or glassware. In some experiments you will need an older person to help you, or at least to stay nearby, so that you don't run the risk of injury.

As you do these experiments, you may discover new questions that you will be able to answer with experiments of your own design. By all means carry out these experiments (with your parents' permission). You are developing the kind of curiosity and ingenuity that is shared by all scientists.

CHAPTER 1

BALANCES ARE FOR WEIGHING

In many experiments it's useful to have a balance to weigh things. You can build a simple balance of your own. But before you do, you might like to try some experiments that will help you understand how a balance works.

A balance, like any other device that turns, rotates about its center of gravity. To find out more about center of gravity try the first experiment.

CENTER OF GRAVITY

Materials: ruler, stiff cardboard, scissors, straight pin, metal washer or nut, thread, pencil

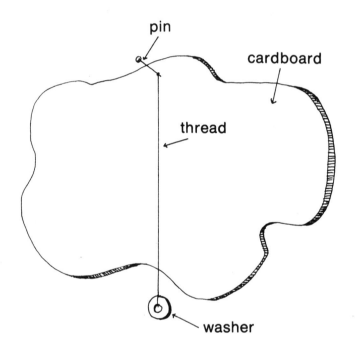

The center of gravity of anything is that point where all the object's weight can be considered to be. It is the point about which the object has no tendency to rotate. It is also the point at which you can pick up the object without having it turn.

12

Try balancing a ruler on your fingertip in different ways: with a flat side, an edge, an end, or a corner resting on your fingertip. It will balance only if your fingertip is under the center of the ruler. In every position the ruler is difficult to balance, but you can see that the higher the center of the ruler is above your fingertip the harder it is to balance.

Cut a sheet of stiff cardboard into an irregular shape. Where is the cardboard's center of gravity? One way to find out is to pin one end of the sheet to a basement wall or to a bulletin board. The cardboard should be free to swing on the pin. Now hang a plumb line from the pin. (You can make a plumb line—a line that points to the center of the earth—by tying a metal washer or nut to a piece of thread.) Draw a line beneath the thread along the cardboard sheet. The line marks the direction to the earth's center.

Now rotate the sheet through 60 to 90 degrees and again pin it at the top edge. Mark another line along the thread. Repeat several times. You will find that the lines all meet at very nearly one point. This point is the center of gravity of the cardboard sheet. To confirm that this point is the center of gravity, take the cardboard off the wall and place that point on your fingertip. Does the cardboard balance at the point you have marked? What happens if you try to balance the sheet at some other point?

YOUR CENTER OF GRAVITY

Materials: wooden block or blackboard eraser, weights, handkerchief

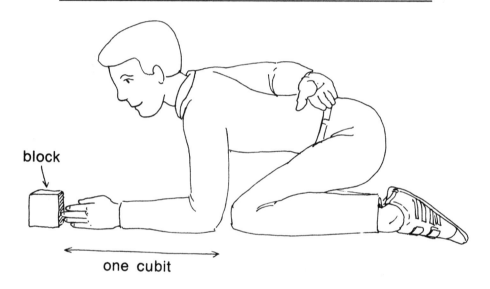

block

one cubit

Where do you think your center of gravity is located?

To find out, lean forward and balance your body on the back of a heavy chair. At what point do you balance?

You can see how important it is to keep your center of gravity above your feet by doing the following experiment. Stand with the entire right side of your body, including the side of your right foot in contact with a wall. Now try to lift your left foot. What happens? Does your body want to rotate about your center of gravity?

14

Now stand with your back against a wall. Be sure your heels are touching the wall. Drop a handkerchief just in front of your toes. Try to pick up the handkerchief without bending your knees or moving your feet. What happens when your center of gravity gets beyond your feet?

Do you think the center of gravity will be different for boys than girls? Here is an experiment to find out.

Get down on your hands and knees and measure one *cubit*, straight out from your knees as shown in the drawing. (A cubit is the length of your forearm from the elbow to the tip of your middle finger.) Place a wooden block or a blackboard eraser on its edge one cubit from your knees. With your hands behind your back, lean forward and try to knock the block over with your nose. Can you do it, or do you fall on your nose instead? Whether you can do it or not has nothing to do with how clever you are; it depends only on how you are built.

Have a number of different people try this experiment. Are girls generally more successful than boys?

As you lean forward, your center of gravity also moves forward. What will happen if your center of gravity gets out beyond your knees?

Repeat the experiment with some weights in your back pockets or on your calves. How will these weights change your center of gravity? Do they make it easier for you to tip the block over?

Do you see now why it's so hard to walk a tightrope or stand up in a small boat? Why is it dangerous to pull a chair away from someone who is in the process of sitting down?

SOME STRANGE BALANCING ACTS

Materials: large coin or washer, dinner forks, soda bottle with cap, knife, apple or potato, pencil, thin cardboard or heavy paper, scissors, clear tape

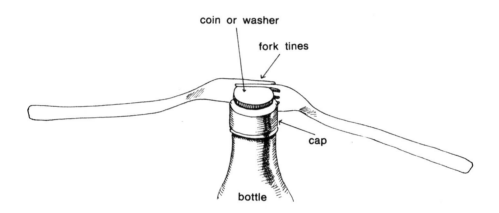

coin or washer

fork tines

cap

bottle

You've seen how unstable an object (including your body) is when its center of gravity is above and beyond its point of support. However, if the center of gravity of an object is below its point of support it will not tip over. You can see this for yourself by building some strange balancing acts.

Insert a large coin or washer between the two upper tines of a pair of forks. (See drawing.) You'll find you can balance the connected objects on the top of a capped soda bottle. What happens if you try this balancing act with the coin between the two lowest tines? Why?

16

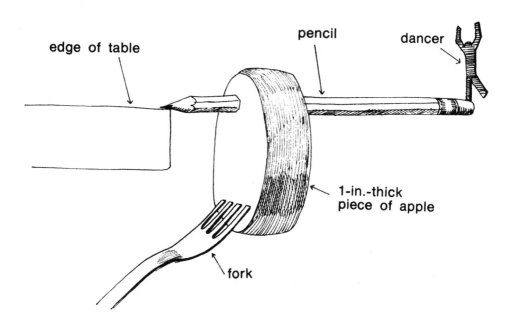

edge of table

pencil

dancer

1-in.-thick
piece of apple

fork

Cut a large slice of apple or potato approximately one inch thick. Carefully push a pencil through the slice and insert a fork below the pencil as shown in the drawing. Balance the object on the edge of a table. If you want, you can make a small cardboard silhouette and attach it to the end of the pencil. A slight downward push on the pencil will provide a dancing silhouette.

With two forks in the slice, you can balance it with the pencil up-right. Turn the cardboard figure 90 degrees and give the pencil a gentle twirl if you want to see your dancer do a pirouette.

Now that you know the secret of strange balancing acts, try making some of your own.

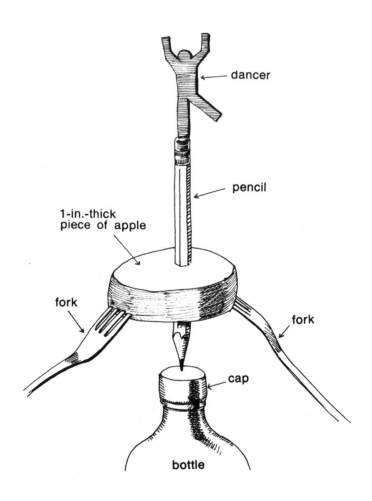

A SODA STRAW BALANCE

Materials: pin or needle, soda straw, paper clips, supports such as cans, glasses or books

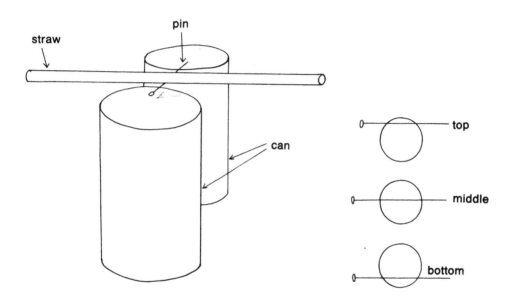

Place the ends of a pin or needle on two supports. Try to balance a soda straw on the pin. Why is it so hard to do?

Now see if you can balance the straw by pushing the pin or needle through the straw. When you succeed, look at the position of the pin. Is it near the middle or near one end of the straw? How about its position from top to bottom of the straw? In which of the three

19

positions shown in the drawing is the straw easiest to balance? Why do you think that's the easiest balancing position? Hint: Where is the straw's center of gravity?

Will the straw remain balanced if you turn it end for end? If you turn it top for bottom?

Hang a paper clip over one end of the balanced straw. (If the clip

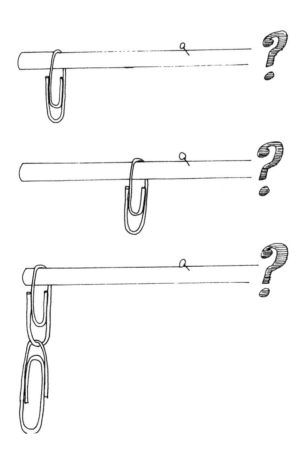

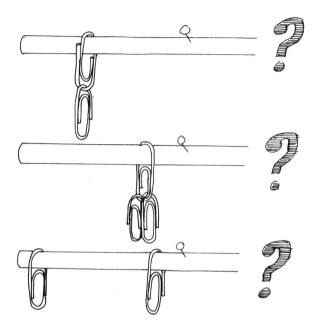

slides along the straw, you may have to pinch the sides of the clip so they rub against the straw.) How can you make the straw balance again without removing the paper clip?

The drawings show just one half of a balanced soda straw. There are clips on the other half, too. What does the other half of the straw look like in each case?

Above are more drawings of the left halves of some balanced soda straws. What does the right half of the straw look like if it has only *one* paper clip on it?

Where would you place two paper clips on the left half of the straw so that it would be impossible to balance the straw with only one paper clip on the right half? Could you make it balance if you moved the *pin* that supports the straw at its center?

21

BUILDING A BALANCE

Materials: ruler, rigid cardboard, pencil, sharp
shears or knife, paper clips, metal washers, string,
paper, supports (cans, glasses, or books),
Styrofoam or aluminum cups, water, eyedropper,
finishing nail

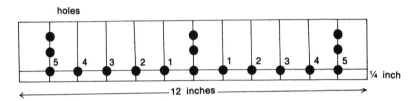

Place a foot-long ruler on a sheet of stiff cardboard. Draw an outline of the ruler with a pencil. Use sharp shears (or ask an adult who
has a sharp knife) to cut out the cardboard section you have marked.
Draw a straight line across the width of the cardboard rectangle at
its exact center. Draw similar lines at one-inch intervals to both the
right and left side of the center line. Then draw a line parallel to the
length of the cardboard one-quarter inch from the edge. Use a small
finishing nail to punch the holes shown in the diagram.

Push the nail through the top center hole. Support the ends of the
nail with two empty cans, glasses, or books. Unbend ten identical
paper clips into hook shapes. Hang them from the ten holes that are
one inch apart along the cardboard beam. If the beam is not level,
use scissors to trim a little off the heavy end. Before you finish
making your balance, take a few minutes to figure out how it works.

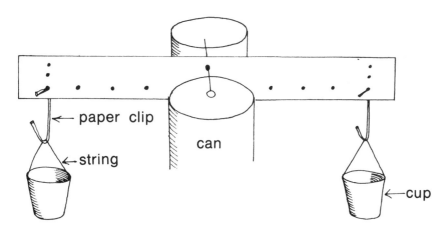

← paper clip

can

←string

←cup

Find about a dozen identical steel washers. Hang one washer on the clip at the number 5 position. Where can you hang a second washer to make the beam level again? Where should you place a single washer on the left side of the beam to balance two washers at the number 2 position on the right side?

Try a variety of combinations of washers and positions that make the balance beam level. Record your results. Then see if you can predict the numbers that belong in the blank spaces in the table following to make the beam balance. Can you find a rule that enables you to predict when the weights at various positions will balance?

From your experiments you can see that in achieving balance, the distance of the weights from the center of the beam is just as important as the number of weights. Have you found a rule yet that allows you to predict whether the beam will balance? If not, see if you can find a way to make the number of washers and their distances from the beam's center equal for both the right and the left sides of the beam. Try adding, dividing, or multiplying the numbers of washers and distances from the center each time the beam is balanced.

Predicting Balancing Positions

Test	Left side Number of Washers	at position	Right side Number of Washers	at position
A	2	5	2	5
B	2	2	1	4
C	5	3	3	—
D	3	—	—	—
E	1	4	2	—
	and		and	
	2	3	—	—
F	2	5	—	3
	and		and	
	3	2	1	4

You might enjoy playing a balance game. Place some washers at different places on one side of the beam. Challenge a friend to make the beam balance by placing washers on the other side. He or she may place the washers at more than one place, but the washers may not be moved once they have been placed on the hooks. Then it's your friend's turn to challenge you.

You've probably found that if the number of washers multiplied by their distance from the center of the beam is the same on both the right and the left sides of the beam, then the beam will balance. That's why most balances are built so that you place the known and unknown weights at equal distances from the center of the beam.

But there is much more to learn about balances. For example, does it make a difference where you place the nail that supports the center beam? To find out, remove all the paper clips except the two in the number 5 holes. Make two pans for your balance using small

24

cups and string or pipe cleaners. Hang the cups from the two paper clips at each end of the beam. If the beam is not level, trim a little cardboard from its heavy end or add clay to the light side.

To test the effect of the position of the nail at the center of the beam you can use water drops as a unit of weight. (You can add the

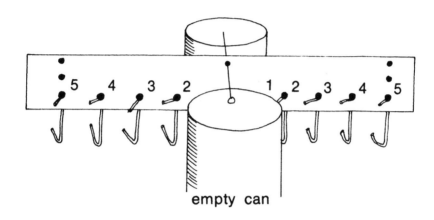

empty can

water with an eyedropper.) With the nail through the upper hole at the beam's center, how many drops of water must you add to one pan before it touches the table? Now dry the pan and repeat the experiment with the nail through the center hole. What happens if you repeat the experiment with the nail through the lowest hole?

With the nail through the top hole, tipping the balance to the right moves the beam's center of gravity to the left side of the line that runs from the support pin to the center of the earth. This makes the beam swing back toward its original position, as you can see in the next drawing.

25

If the nail is through the bottom hole, tipping the beam to the right moves the beam's center of gravity to the right, too. This causes the beam to continue turning to the right.

As you have seen, the balance is very stable (well balanced) when the pin is through the top hole. However, it is not very sensitive; that is, it doesn't move very far when a small amount of weight is added to one side. If the nail is through the bottom hole, the balance is so sensitive that it is useless; it just swings all the way to the heavy side.

Put the nail through the center hole. Now test the stability and sensitivity of the balance when the *pans* are suspended from the top, middle, and lower holes at the ends of the beam. Which arrangement is most sensitive? Which is unstable? Which is least sensitive?

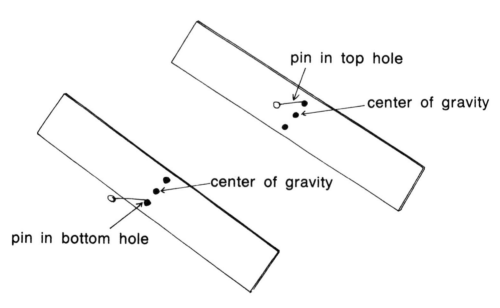

What will happen to the sensitivity of your balance if you move the pans closer to the center of the beam?

If you place several washers in each pan, will it affect the sensitivity of the balance?

How could you build a better balance?

Now use your balance to weigh some things. Which is heavier, a penny or a dime? A nickel or two dimes?

If you have identical paper clips, you can use them as a unit of weight. For example, how many paper clips does a penny weigh? How about a washer? How could you weigh something that weighs less than a paper clip? How could you weigh something that weighs between three and four paper clips?

CHAPTER 2

WEIGHING IN THE KITCHEN

HOW STICKY ARE DIFFERENT LIQUIDS?

Materials: balance, plastic plate, straight pin, sharp scissors, pliers, paper clips, water, flat container for water, alcohol, soap, cooking oil, ruler

You can measure the stickiness or "hold togetherness" of various liquids by measuring how much pull (in paper clips) is required to pull the liquid apart. To measure the pull, you can use the balance you built, but first you'll need to make a plate that will adhere to liquids. That's easy to do. Just cut a two-inch square from a plastic cover such as the ones found on coffee cans, margarine tubs, and artificial topping containers. Push a straight pin through the center of the square. If you find this difficult, ask an adult to help you heat the end of the pin with a match while you hold it with pliers. The hot pin will then go through the plastic very easily. Use the pliers to bend the sharp end of the pin into a loop so you can hang it from one end of the balance with string or a paper clip. If the beam is not level, add a little clay to one side of the beam, or slide an opened paper clip along the light side of the beam until it is level.

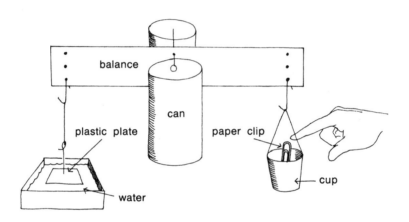

Once the beam is level, place the plastic square on the surface of some tap water in a clean container. How many paper clips, gently placed in the cup on the other side of the beam, are required to pull the water apart? (If you look closely, you'll see that there is water on the plastic plate. This shows that the water pulled apart.) Repeat the experiment again to see if you get similar results. If you need fractions of a paper clip, you can hang an opened paper clip on the beam and slide it from the center outward until the beam is level. Since the beam is divided into fifths, each fifth you slide the clip is equal to 0.2 paper clip. Halfway between the third and fourth holes is equivalent to 0.7 paper clip.

Add some soap to the water. Does soapy water pull apart more easily than plain water? How about alcohol? Cooking oil?

If you try these other liquids, be sure to clean and dry the plate and the container that holds the liquid before each experiment.

Will the shape of the plate affect the results of your experiment? How about the surface area of the plate? When you change the shape of the plate, what should you do about the surface area? Do experiments to answer these questions. What do you find?

THE PAPER TOWEL SOAK-UP

Materials: paper towels, balance, paper clips, a nickel

Remove the pans from your balance and hang half a paper towel on the paper clip hook at the left end of the beam. Hang paper clips on the other end in order to find the weight of the towel. How many paper clips does the half-towel weigh? Now wet the towel. When the excess water has dripped off, weigh the wet towel. How much water, in paper clips, did the towel absorb?

To find the weight in grams you need to know the weight of a paper clip in grams. You can find out very easily by using paper clips to weigh a nickel. A nickel weighs 5 grams. How many grams of water did the paper towel absorb?

Watch the balance beam as the towel dries. How long does it take for the towel to lose a paper clip's weight of water? What can you do to make the towel dry faster?

DENSITY: A MEASURE OF COMPACTNESS

Materials: balance, paper clips, small wood block, clay, medicine cup(s), rubbing alcohol, salt, water, cooking oil, ruler

---

A piece of gold weighs more than seven times as much as a piece of aluminum of the same size (volume). This tells you that gold is much more compact than aluminum. Scientists say that gold is more *dense* than aluminum. If you divide the weight of anything by its volume, the number you get is called the density of that material. For example, a cubic foot of water weighs 62.4 pounds. Therefore, its density is 62.4 pounds per cubic foot. One cubic centimeter of gold weighs 19.3 grams; its density is 19.3g/cm3.

You can find out which of two materials is more dense by placing equal volumes of the two substances on opposite sides of an equal arm balance. Try it with a wooden block and a piece of clay that you have made equal in size and shape to the wood. Which block is more dense?

If you change the shape of the clay block, will its density change? How can you check the accuracy of your prediction?

With a medicine cup you can compare the weights of equal volumes of different liquids. Is rubbing alcohol more or less dense than water? How about cooking oil? Salt water?

How could you measure the actual densities of these liquids in grams per cubic centimeter (g/cm3) or grams per milliliter (g/mL)? (A milliliter and a cubic centimeter are the same volume.)

DROPS AND DENSITIES

Materials: hot water, cold water, food coloring, eyedropper, vials (pill bottles), drinking glasses or jars, salt (preferably kosher), various liquids and solids

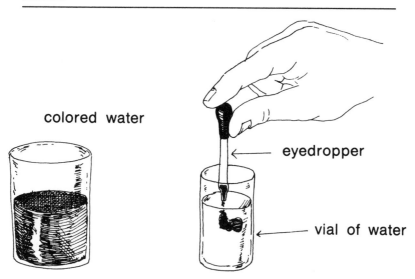

colored water

eyedropper

vial of water

There is another way to compare the densities of liquids. What do you think will happen if you *slowly* squeeze a drop of cooking oil from the end of a medicine dropper into the middle of a container of water? Will the drop go up or down, or will it remain in the middle? What will happen if you squeeze a drop of water into the center of some cooking oil?

The drop test is a very sensitive way to compare densities. To see this for yourself, use a drop of food coloring to color some hot tap water. Now slowly squeeze a drop of the hot colored water into a container of cold tap water. What does your experiment tell you about the density of hot water as compared with that of cold water?

Repeat the experiment, but this time color the cold water and squeeze a drop of it into some hot water. What do you predict will happen to the drop?

Try the test with liquids that differ only slightly in density. Fill four identical glasses three-fourths full of cold tap water. Add one table-spoonful of salt to the first glass of water. (If possible, use kosher salt; it makes a clear solution because it has no additives.) Add two tablespoonfuls to the second glass, and three to the third. Stir all three liquids until the salt is dissolved. Add several drops of food coloring to each liquid. You might color one liquid red, another blue, and the third green. The fourth, unsalted water, can be left uncolored.

To determine the density order of the four liquids, from least dense to most dense, put samples of the four liquids into separate pill bottles or vials and, using a medicine dropper, add drops of one to the others. How many combinations are there to try? Which test, balance or drop, do you think is more sensitive?

In addition to the three salt solutions and water, you might like to test some other liquids and add them to your density list. You could try alcohol, cooking oil, sugar water, apple juice, milk, and many other liquids.

You could also add solids to your list. Are all solids denser than all liquids? How about wood? Clay? Aluminum? Other solids? Where does each solid fit into your density order?

HOW MUCH OF THE FOOD YOU EAT IS WATER?

Materials: balance, paper clips, oven, various kinds of food, small aluminum pans

Take some small pieces of different foods: bread, potato, carrot, celery, and cereal, for example. Weigh each food and record your results. Place the foods in separate small aluminum pans. Put the pans in a warm oven for several hours. Heat will dry the food. Weigh the food again and continue heating and weighing until there is no further change in weight. Record the dry weight of each piece of food. Then calculate what percentage of the food was water. For example, if a piece of bread weighed 6 paper clips before drying and 2 paper clips afterward, its water content was 4 paper clips. Thus, the water made up four-sixths, or 67 percent, of the bread.

Which of the foods you tested contains the largest percentage of water? Which food was the driest?

SOME DENSITY INVESTIGATIONS

Materials: Alka-Seltzer, water, soda bottle, tire pump, balloons, tie bands, stone, steel washers, container, balance, various metals, clay, soap, bathtub

• As you might guess, gases have very low densities. But do all gasses have the same density? To find out, get two iden-

35

tical balloons and tie bands. Use the tie bands to hang the balloons from opposite ends of your balance. Be sure the beam is level.

Prepare some carbon dioxide gas by breaking three or four Alka-Seltzer tablets into small pieces and adding them to about an inch of water in a small soda bottle. Attach a balloon to the neck of the bottle to collect the carbon dioxide. When the reaction between water and Alka-Seltzer is over (the bubbles will stop), carefully remove the balloon. Use a tie band to seal the balloon and hang it from the same end of the balance where it was before. Use a tire pump to put an equal volume of air in another identical balloon. Close it off with a tie band. Use the balance to see if one gas is denser than the other.

Replace the pump air in one balloon with your own lung air. Which is denser, lung air or carbon dioxide? Lung air or pump air? Is the air that you exhale pure carbon dioxide? How do you know?

- Which is more dense, a stone or steel washers? To find out you'll need to determine the weight per volume for each solid, or compare the weights of equal volumes. (Hint: An object that sinks in water displaces a volume of water equal to its own volume.)

  Use the same method to compare, or actually measure, the densities of steel, aluminum, copper, brass, and lead.

- You have seen that both clay and steel sink in water. This tells you these solids are denser than water; yet, steel ships float. Even the concrete boats used in World War II floated. If you can make a piece of clay float, you'll probably be able to explain why steel or concrete boats float. Try it! Can you

36

explain why even boats made of concrete can be made to float?

- Next time you go swimming, try to float on the surface on your back. What happens to your position in the water when you inhale a deep breath? What happens when you exhale? How do you explain your observations?
- Which is densest, you, your bath soap, or your bath water? Which is least dense? How do you know?

HOW MUCH DOES AIR WEIGH?

Materials: balance, plastic bag, tie bands, paper clips

Use a tie band to hang an empty plastic bag from one end of your balance. How much does the bag weigh? Swing the bag swiftly through the air as you hold it open. Use the same tie band to close off the air trapped in the bag. Then weigh the bag and the air. How much does the air appear to weigh? Are you surprised by your results?

To help you understand why air appears to be weightless try the next two experiments.

WEIGHING WATER IN WATER

Materials: balance, balloon, tie band, water, salt
(preferably kosher), alcohol, jar, paper clips,
pitcher or measuring cup

After you have leveled your balance beam, carefully fill a balloon with water. Let the bottom of the balloon rest on the kitchen counter as you slowly pour in tap water from a small pitcher or measuring cup. Wait a few moments for air bubbles to leave. Then tie off the balloon with a tie band being careful not to form any air pockets in the balloon. Hang the water balloon from one end of the balance. Place a large jar of water beneath the balloon and raise it until the balloon is submerged. You will find that the water balloon now appears to be weightless. In fact, if you were careful not to get any air bubbles in the balloon, the water-filled balloon will neither sink nor float when released in the jar.

What happens when you place the water balloon in a jar of salt water? In a jar of alcohol? In what gas did you weigh air?

WEIGHING SOLIDS IN LIQUIDS

Materials: clay or metal washer, tie band, balance, water, salt, alcohol, paper clips

Weigh a piece of clay or a metal washer by attaching it to one end of your balance with a tie band. Then reweigh the solid while it is submerged in a jar of water. What happens to the apparent weight of the solid?

Do you think the solid will appear to weigh more or will it appear to weigh less if weighed in salt water? If weighed in alcohol? Test your predictions with an experiment.

Would carbon dioxide appear to weigh more in air or in a vacuum? How much do you think carbon dioxide would appear to weigh in an atmosphere of carbon dioxide?

CHAPTER 3

HOT
AND COLD
AND WET

You've already seen that much of the food we eat is really water. Now you'll discover how water becomes rain and fog. You will find also that even on a clear day there is water all around us.

A FOGGY BOTTLE

Materials: jar, ice cube, hot water

Find a jar with a mouth slightly smaller than the length of an ice cube. Fill the jar with *hot* water; then pour out all but about an inch of the water. Place an ice cube on the mouth of the jar and hold the jar up to the light. Do you see thin streams of fog forming where the warm air in the jar meets the ice?

HUMIDITY

Materials: shiny metal can, spoon for stirring, warm water, ice

In the last experiment you made fog. But where did the fog come from—the ice or the warm air? Repeat the experiment, but this time wrap the ice cube in a small, thin plastic bag.

The fact that fog still forms shows that the moisture did not come from the ice. It must have come from water in the warm air above the hot water.

Just as sugar dissolves in water and cannot be seen, so water dissolves in air. And, like particles of sugar, the particles of water are so small they can't be seen. You may know that more sugar will dissolve in hot water than in cold water. Perhaps more water can dissolve in hot air than in cold air.

At any temperature there is a limit to the amount of sugar that will dissolve in a liter of water. When this limit is reached, we say the solution is saturated. If the temperature of a saturated sugar solution decreases, the water cannot hold as much sugar. The sugar in excess of saturation falls out of solution. Is the same true of water in the atmosphere?

To test this idea, slowly lower the temperature of some warm water in a *shiny* metal can. You can do this by adding small pieces of ice to the water as you stir it. If our idea is correct, water should fall out of the air (condense) when the air is cold enough to form a saturated solution of water in air. Look for signs of moisture on the outside of the can as the temperature falls. Can you find evidence to support our idea?

In the summertime you've probably seen moisture on the *outside* of a cold pitcher of iced tea or milk. How do you explain such moisture? Where have you seen condensed moisture in the wintertime?

ABSOLUTE HUMIDITY

Materials: thermometer and materials used in previous experiment

The water dissolved in air is called humidity. The quantity of water dissolved in one cubic meter of air is called the *absolute humidity*. It can be measured using a method similar to the one you used in the previous experiment. Just repeat that experiment, but this time stir the water with a thermometer as you cool it. Record the temperature at which you first see moisture condensing on the can. This temperature is called the *dew point*.

Once you have found the dew point, you can use the table on the next page to determine the absolute humidity. The table gives the maximum amount of water that can be dissolved in one cubic meter of air at a given temperature.

You know the dew point; therefore you know the temperature at which the air in contact with the can is saturated with water vapor. For example, suppose the air in the room you are working in is 68°F (20°C), and you find the dew point to be 50°F (10°C). From the table you see that the air holds 9.3g/m3.

At 20°C the air could hold 17.1 grams of moisture per cubic meter. But in our example it contains only 9.3 grams of the 17.1 grams it could hold. Therefore, it contains only 9.3/17.1 or 54 percent of the moisture required for saturation. This ratio—the water vapor present in the air compared to the total vapor the air could hold if saturated—when expressed as a percentage, is called the relative humidity.

Grams of Moisture in One Cubic Meter of Saturated Air at Various Temperatures

Temperature	Water Vapor (grams)	Temperature	Water Vapor (grams)
32°F (0°C)	4.8	68°F (20°C)	17.1
41°F (5°C)	6.8	77°F (25°C)	22.8
50°F (10°C)	9.3	86°F (30°C)	30.0
59°F (15°C)	12.7	95°F (35°C)	39.2

Use the dew point and the temperature of the air to determine the absolute and relative humidity in your kitchen. Repeat the experiment in your bathroom just after you take a shower. Which room do you think will have the greater *absolute* humidity? The greater *relative* humidity?

Try the same experiment in various parts of your house and outdoors. Try it on clear, cloudy, and rainy days. Try it at different times of the year. What changes in absolute and relative humidity do you find?

EVAPORATION

Materials: water, drinking glasses, marking pen, electric fan

---

Most of the moisture in air comes from lakes and oceans through a process called evaporation.

To see what evaporation is, fill five identical drinking glasses about three-fourths full of water. Line the glasses up and be sure they all contain the same volume. Make a mark on each glass at the water level.

Put one glass in a warm, open place. (On a radiator might be a good location.) Put another in a cool but not freezing open place. (Near a window in the wintertime would be good.) Leave the third one at room temperature. Place the fourth glass near the third, but cover it with a small plate or saucer. The fifth glass should be placed in front of an electric fan if you have one.

Mark the water levels in each glass over a period of several days. Which glass seemed to lose the most water? Which one lost none? What effect did temperature have on the water lost?

The escape of water from its surface is called evaporation. Where do you think the water goes? What was the purpose of the covered glass in this experiment?

EVAPORATION IS COOL

Materials: thermometer, water, electric fan, thin cloth

On a hot summer day what can you do to cool off if you don't have an air conditioner?

Outside you might look for a place where there is a breeze; indoors you might turn on a fan. In a moving car you could open a window and let the air flow over you. All these ways of getting cool involve moving air. Is moving air really cooler than still air?

To find out, place a thermometer in a room. After a few minutes record the temperature. Now place a fan in front of the thermometer. Does the temperature go up, down, or remain the same? Is moving air cooler than still air?

Swimming is another way to get cool. In fact, when you come out of the water and stand in a breeze, you may feel cold and start to shiver. You know the moving air isn't cold; cooling off must have something to do with your wet skin. Could the evaporation of water from your skin make you feel cold?

You know from the previous experiment that water evaporates faster when air is moving over it.

To see if rapid evaporation can cool a moist object, soak a strip of thin cloth in water. Wrap the cloth around the bulb of a thermometer. When the liquid in the thermometer tube stops moving, note the temperature. Now, hold the thermometer in front of a spinning fan or swing it through the air for a few minutes. What happens to the temperature?

Evaporation happens because the fastest-moving molecules in a liquid are constantly leaving the surface to become a gas. When water evaporates, the gas is the water vapor that makes up the humidity in the air. Because the fastest-moving molecules are the warmest ones, the ones that remain behind in the liquid are the cooler ones: hence the liquid becomes cooler as it evaporates.

COOLING AND THE RATE OF EVAPORATION

Materials: hot water, three aluminum pie pans, cooking oil, newspaper, three thermometers, electric fan

Knowing that a liquid cools as it evaporates, try to predict how the *rate* of evaporation will affect the temperature of an evaporating liquid.

To check up on your prediction, pour equal amounts of hot water into three identical aluminum pie pans. Place the pans on folded newspapers for insulation. Submerge a thermometer in each pan. To keep the evaporation rate near zero in one pan, add a few drops of cooking oil to cover the water. Leave a second pan undisturbed. To increase the rate of evaporation in a third pan, use an electric fan to blow air across it, but make sure the air from the fan doesn't go near the other two pans.

Record the temperature in each pan at one-minute intervals for a few minutes. In which pan does the water cool fastest? Did you predict correctly?

Can you explain why sweating keeps you cool?

47

RAIN IN THE KITCHEN

Materials: tea kettle, ice water, water, pan, stove
(Be sure you have your parent's permission to use the stove.)

You've seen that warm air holds more moisture than cold air. You've seen also that when the temperature falls below the dew point, water vapor in the air begins to fall out of solution.

Using these principles, you can make it rain in your kitchen. Heat a tea kettle of water to boiling on the kitchen stove. (*Be careful in using the stove. Be sure to turn it off when you are finished.*) Hold a pan of ice in the clear stream of steam emerging from the tea kettle. Can you make it "rain" from the bottom of the cold pan?

MAKE A CLOUD

Materials: cold water, glass bottle, one-hole rubber stopper, air pump, thermometer, wooden matches, safety glasses, an adult to help

The formation of rain droplets in the atmosphere is more complex than the "kitchen rain" you produced. Tiny droplets of rain form on minute particles of salt or dust that serve as condensation nuclei. And the water vapor is cooled by its expansion as it ascends into the upper atmosphere where the pressure is less.

You can see this effect for yourself. Put some cold water in a clear glass bottle. *Be sure the bottle has no cracks.* Shake the bottle with your hand over its mouth to saturate the enclosed air with water vapor. Have an adult blow out a burning match and let the smoke escape into the mouth of the inverted bottle. The smoke particles will serve as condensation nuclei so that droplets of water can form as the water vapor cools. To cool the air and vapor, connect an air pump to a one-hole rubber stopper and put the stopper into the bottle's mouth. Put on safety glasses now. Pump air into the bottle until you pop the stopper. The expansion of the pressurized air will cool the vapor, causing it to condense into tiny droplets that form a cloud inside the bottle.

Just as expansion causes a gas to cool, so compression will cause a gas to become warmer. To see this effect, use an air pump to force compressed air across the bulb of a thermometer. What happens to the temperature?

In a diesel engine the compression of the fuel vapor produces a temperature high enough to ignite the vapor. As a result, diesel engines, unlike gasoline engines, do not have spark plugs.

AIR PRESSURE

Materials: water, pail or sink, water glass, index card, one-gallon metal can with cap or rubber stopper to fit opening, cardboard sheet or heatproof mat, pot holders or glove, stove, an adult to help

---

To see that air really does exert a pressure, try these experiments.

- Fill a pail or sink with water. Submerge a drinking glass and fill it. Turn the glass under water so that it is upside down, and slowly lift it until most of it, but not the open end, is out of the water. As you can see, the water in the glass is well above the water level in the sink. Normally, gravity would cause water to fall from the glass. What's keeping the water up?
- Fill a glass to the brim with water. Place an index card on the glass. Put your hand on top of the card and invert the glass of water over the sink. Remove your hand. Why don't the card and water fall from the glass?
- Here is an even more dramatic experiment to show the presence of air pressure. In this experiment you will get rid of the air that is normally inside a container. Then you'll be able to see the effect of the force that air pressure exerts when there is little or no opposing force.

  Ask an adult to help you with this experiment; he or she will enjoy it as much as you will.

Take a one-gallon metal can like the ones that paint thinner and duplicating-machine fluid come in. If the can's screw-on cap is missing, use a rubber stopper that fits the opening in the can.

Rinse the can thoroughly to remove any flammable liquid that might remain. Pour a cup of water into the can. Leave the top of the can open and heat the can on the stove. Steam from the boiling water will drive air out of the can. Let the water boil for several minutes to be sure that most of the air is gone.

Using gloves or pot holders to protect your hands, remove the can from the heat and place it on a thick piece of cardboard or a heatproof mat. *Immediately* seal the can with its screw-on cap or a rubber stopper.

As the can cools, the steam will condense leaving the can very nearly empty. Watch how the air outside the can, unopposed now by air that is normally inside, pushes inward on all sides of the can. You'll be amazed by the strength of air!

HOW FAR AWAY IS THE STORM?

Materials: watch or clock with a second hand

You probably know that thunder is caused by the expansion of air heated by a lightning stroke. But the speed of sound (1/5 mile per second or 331 meters per second) is negligible compared with the speed of light (186,000 miles per second or 300,000 kilometers per second). That is why you see the lightning before you hear the thunder.

Because the light from lightning reaches your eyes almost instantaneously, you can use the time delay between the sight of lightning and the sound of the thunder it creates to determine how far away the lightning was. Count the number of seconds between the lightning and the thunder. Since sound travels 1/5 mile per second or 1/3 kilometer per second, it takes 5 seconds to go one mile and 3 seconds to go one kilometer. If you divide the number of seconds between lightning and thunder by 5, you will have the distance to the lightning in miles. How would you find the distance in kilometers?

Repeat the experiment every few minutes. Is the storm approaching or moving away?

CHAPTER 4

FROM CEILING TO FLOOR: THE SCIENCE OF FALLING OBJECTS

It was Galileo, in the sixteenth century, who first studied falling bodies scientifically—that is, by doing experiments with falling things, not just talking about them.

You, too, can experiment with falling objects. But be careful that you don't fall with them.

DIFFERENT WEIGHT, DIFFERENT FALL?

Materials: several balls of different weight such as tennis, baseball, and lacrosse balls, paper, book

book

paper

Hold a heavy ball and a light ball at the same height. Predict which ball will hit the floor first if you release both of them at the same time. Repeat the experiment several times. Galileo found that objects with different weights fall together. Do you agree? Drop the two balls at the same time from various equal heights. Do they still fall side by side?

Now drop a ball and a piece of paper from the same height at the same time. Do they fall together?

Repeat the experiment, but this time crumple the paper into a tight ball. What do you find about their falling rates now?

Place a sheet of paper on the cover of a book that is larger than the paper. Drop the book and paper. Why do they fall together?

Galileo guessed that the small force between the air and a light piece of paper would be enough to cause the paper to fall more slowly than a much heavier object. But, he argued, in a vacuum both paper and ball would fall together. Years later, when scientists were able to make a vacuum, a coin and a feather were found to fall side by side.

During a moon walk, American astronauts tested Galileo's hypothesis by dropping a hammer and a feather. In the airless space above the moon's surface, the two objects fell at the same rate, just as Galileo had predicted they would.

THE SPEED OF A FALLING BALL

Materials: ball, yardstick or meterstick

If you count from one to five as fast as you can, you'll find it takes just about one second. Try it ten times in a row and you'll see that just about ten seconds have elapsed.

You can use this method of timing to estimate fractions of a second. For example, if you start counting as fast as you can when an event begins and you have counted to three when the event ends, then the event took approximately 3/5 (0.6) of a second.

55

Drop a ball from a height of one yard or one meter. At the moment you release the ball begin counting as fast as you can. Stop counting when the ball hits the floor. Repeat the experiment several times until you're quite sure how long it takes the ball to fall. You'll find it's just over 0.4 seconds; that is, you'll be just starting to say "three" when the ball hits the floor.

How far will the ball have to travel to make its fall take twice as long—about 0.9 second? Does a height of 2 yards or meters work? If it did, what would it tell you about the ball's falling speed?

After doing an experiment similar to the one you have just tried, Galileo was convinced that falling objects do not travel at constant speed. He also realized, as you probably have, that the time intervals required for objects to fall small distances were too small to measure accurately. To overcome this difficulty he devised an ingenious means of diluting gravity. Using this device he found that a ball had to fall 4 meters to take twice the time required to fall 1 meter. Do you agree?

DILUTING GRAVITY

Materials: heavy toy truck, smooth board, spring scale or long rubber band or a chain of short rubber bands, two yardsticks, a large marble, more rubber bands, pieces of wood or metal for separating yardsticks, book or block

---

Galileo believed that bodies fall toward the earth because of a force we call gravity—an attraction that earth has for all matter. No one knows why there is such a force. There are certainly no strings or ropes connecting you or any object to the center of the earth; yet, the force is there and we all feel it.

To dilute the force of gravity Galileo built an inclined plane. You can see for yourself that the force of gravity is diluted by such a plane. Hang a heavy toy truck from a spring scale, a long rubber band, or a chain of short rubber bands hooked together. Determine how much the spring or rubber is stretched by the weight of the truck. Then place the truck against a long board and slowly lower the board from a vertical toward a horizontal position thus making it an inclined plane. What happens to the force needed to move the truck along the board as the angle between the board and the floor becomes smaller? Do you see why Galileo thought of an inclined plane as a way of diluting the force of gravity?

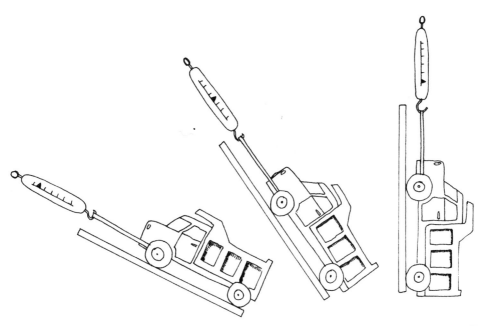

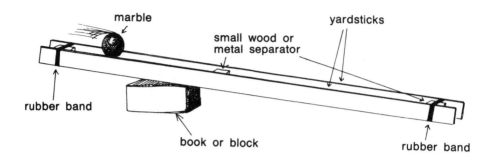

To see how much easier it is to measure time when gravity is diluted, build the inclined plane shown in the drawing using two yardsticks. Separate the sticks with small pieces of wood or metal so that a large marble will roll easily down the incline when one end is raised about 2 inches above the floor or counter.

How long does it take the marble to roll from the 2-inch line to the 10-inch line, a distance of 8 inches? You can time the descent with a stopwatch or by counting to five very fast as you did before. According to Galileo, how long should it take the marble to roll 32 inches, from the 2-inch line to the 34-inch line? Try it. How long did it take? What was the average speed of the marble, in inches per second, while it was rolling the first 8 inches? What was its average speed for 32 inches? What is happening to the speed of the marble as it "falls" along the incline?

WHAT'S YOUR REACTION TIME?

Materials: dollar bill, yardstick or meterstick

Offer to let your friends keep a dollar if they can catch it before it falls through their fingers. It's quite certain that you'll keep your dollar. A dollar is about 6 inches (15 centimeters) long. Have the person trying to catch the bill hold his or her thumb and index finger about 2 inches above the bottom edge of the bill before you release it. Your friend must react before the dollar falls 4 inches—a period of only 0.15 second. Few people, if any, can see the bill start to fall and then react fast enough to catch it.

To test someone's reaction time, have that person place his or her fingers loosely around the bottom of a yardstick that you hold in a vertical position. Tell the person to catch the yardstick as quickly as possible after it starts to fall.

From the table below, you can determine the person's reaction time.

Reaction Times on the Basis
of the Distance a Yardstick Falls before Being Caught

If the yardstick falls this distance, in inches, before being caught . . .	the person's reaction time, in seconds, is
6	0.177
12	0.25
18	0.306
24	0.353
30	0.395
36	0.433

FALLING SIDEWAYS: PENDULUMS IN MOTION

Materials: metal washers, string or thread, paper clips or tongue depressor or popsicle stick, yardstick, tape, clock or watch with second hand

Fashion a pendulum by tying a metal washer to a long piece of thread. Slide the upper end of the thread into a slit in a tongue depressor or attach it to a paper clip. Then tape the paper clip or tongue depressor to the top of a door frame as in the drawing.

Pull the washer to one side and release it from a known height above the floor. Watch it make one complete cycle, or period—over and back. To what height above the floor does it rise on the other end of its swing?

Galileo noticed that a pendulum bob (the weight at the end of the string) rises to very nearly the same height on one side of its swing as it does on the other. Of course, the swing gradually diminishes and eventually stops, but Galileo believed that if there were no friction, the bob would continue to swing back and forth forever. From this he reasoned that if a block or ball were to slide down a frictionless incline, it would rise to the same height on a second incline, just as a pendulum bob does in its swing. If the second incline were made longer and less steep, the ball would travel farther before starting its return. If there were no second incline, but only a horizontal plane, the ball, reasoned Galileo, would continue to move indefinitely. "After all," he asked, "what force would stop it if there were no friction?"

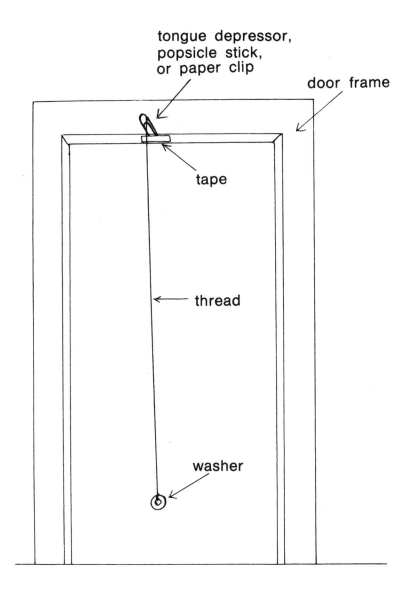

tongue depressor,
popsicle stick,
or paper clip

door frame

tape

thread

washer

It was Galileo who first realized a body in motion will continue to move at the same speed unless some force changes its motion. Usually, there are frictional forces that cause a body to slow down. Of course, he argued, if a body is at rest (speed = 0), it will stay in place unless acted upon by some force.

In Galileo's time there were no clocks outside of church towers, but he realized that a pendulum could be used to keep very good time. To see why, set your pendulum in motion, and measure its period—the time it takes the pendulum to make one complete swing, over and back. It's difficult to measure a single period so use a clock or watch to time 10 or 100 swings, then divide the number of seconds by 10 or 100. For instance if the pendulum makes 100 swings in two minutes (120 seconds), its period is 120 seconds/100, which is 1.20 seconds. If it makes 100 swings in only one minute, its period is 0.60 second (60/100).

Determine the period of your pendulum. Then let it swing for several minutes and determine its period again. Has it changed? Do you see why Galileo regarded the pendulum as a good way to keep time? Have you ever seen a clock with a pendulum?

Measure the length of your pendulum from the point of support at the top to the center of the washer. Add a second washer to the bob so that its weight doubles, but keep the length exactly the same. Does the weight of the pendulum bob affect its period?

Does the length of the pendulum affect its period? How can you find out?

How about the amplitude of its swing—the distance that it moves—does that affect its period?

PENDULUMS THAT DANCE AND TWIST

Materials: pencil or thin stick, string, steel washers, tape, chair or table or door frame

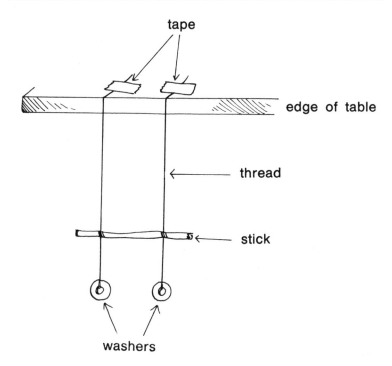

Pendulums are all around us. Watch a hook swinging from a crane. You can determine its length quite accurately by timing its swing. Watch a hanging plant or wind chimes in a breeze. Or watch the slow swing of a giraffe's or an elephant's long legs as it walks.

63

Compare their period with the rapid natural motion of a small dog's legs. Compare the gaits of a professional basketball center and a young child.

Hang two pendulums of equal length (about 2 feet), and with equal-weight bobs, side by side from a chair, tabletop, or door frame. They should be about 6 inches apart. As you can see, they will swing with the same period.

Connect the two pendulums with a thin stick or pencil. Wind each pendulum's string around the stick once about a foot above the bobs. Pull one bob to the side and let go. Notice how it transfers its motion to the other bob because of their connection.

To make the pendulums do a twisting dance, move the stick down closer to the bobs. What happens now after you start one pendulum?

What happens if you change the weight of one bob by adding more washers?

THINGS TEND TO STAY PUT

Materials: 3-by-5-inch index card or playing card, cup or glass, coin, water, plastic dishes, silverware, newspaper or smooth cloth

The idea that objects at rest tend to remain at rest is one that Galileo probably came to by doing experiments like these.

- Place an index card or playing card over the top of a cup or drinking glass. Put a coin or washer on the center of the card. With a sharp flick of your finger, drive the card off the cup.

Or, if you find it easier to do, give the card a quick pull. What happens to the coin? Does it tend to remain at rest?

- Place the index card on the edge of a table or counter. About one-third of the card should project out beyond the edge. Put some water in a plastic cup or glass and place it on the other two-thirds of the card. Give the card a *quick* pull toward you. What happens to the water-filled cup? Does it stay in place?

- Now that you're confident that things do tend to stay in place, you may be ready to try a "trick" you've probably seen on television or in a movie. Cover part of a table or counter with a newspaper or smooth cloth. Set the table with a plate, cup and saucer, and silverware. With a sharp yank you can pull the "tablecloth" out from under the utensils, leaving them undisturbed on the table. (It's a good idea to use plastic dishes until you're an expert at this experiment.)

THINGS IN MOTION CONTINUE IN MOTION

Materials: balloon, 1/16-inch bit and drill, 3-inch square of 1/4-inch plywood or Masonite, sandpaper, empty spool that formerly held thread, balloon, glue

As his first law of motion Sir Isaac Newton used Galileo's idea that the motion of a body (at rest or moving) tends to be maintained. This is commonly known as the law of inertia—the idea that the motion of a body can be changed only by applying a force, a push or a pull.

You've seen that bodies at rest tend to stay at rest unless a force

65

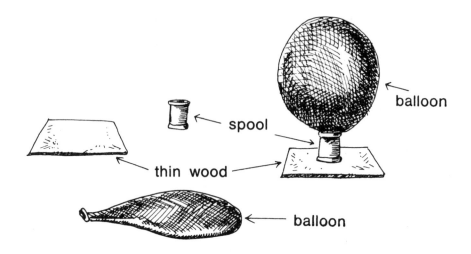

is applied, but it's more difficult to demonstrate that a body in motion tends to maintain its motion. Usually, frictional forces cause a body to slow down and stop unless we apply a force greater than or equal to the friction. That's why your moving bicycle will stop unless you pedal; it's why a car comes to a stop unless we use the engine to keep turning the wheels.

A pendulum's motion is nearly frictionless, but it's a back-and-forth motion. By building an "air car" you can see virtually frictionless motion along a straight line.

To build such a car, ask an adult to help you drill a 1/16-inch hole in the very center of a 1/4-inch-thick piece of plywood or Masonite. The thin piece of wood can be either a square about 2½ to 3 inches on a side or a circle with a similar diameter.

Use sandpaper to make one side of the wood very smooth. The outside edges of the wood should be sanded to round them off.

Glue one end of an empty spool (there may be one in your sewing kit) to the unsanded side of the square or disk. Be sure the hole in the spool is directly over the hole in the wood.

66

When the glue is thoroughly dry, attach an inflated balloon to the spool and place the car on a Formica counter. Air emerging from beneath the wood will provide a thin air space between wood and counter. Give the car a push. Notice how it moves with no sign of slowing down unless it comes to a hill.

You see evidence of inertia in your daily life. If you are riding in a car, train, or bus that stops suddenly, you tend to keep moving forward. In an automobile you feel the seat belt, which is attached to the car, holding you back when this happens. That's why seat belts are helpful in accidents; they prevent people from continuing to move, through a windshield, for example.

Ice on a highway reduces the friction between tires and road so that cars will often continue to move straight when they come to a curve and so slide off the road.

On a seesaw, you tend to keep going up after your partner's end of the board hits the ground. When it's your turn to go down, you feel the bump as you tend to keep going after your end of the seesaw hits the ground.

FALLING AT CONSTANT SPEED

Materials: tall jar, water, salt, egg, baster or funnel and tubing that fits funnel spout, food coloring

You have seen that when an object falls, its speed increases; it accelerates like a car that is speeding up. Since the motion of a falling body is changing, there must be a force acting on it; otherwise, it would continue to move with the same speed. But you have also seen that a piece of paper does not fall as fast as a ball. Friction with

67

the air seems to slow its fall. In fact, any object falling through the air will eventually stop accelerating and reach a steady speed—its terminal velocity. When sky divers jump from an airplane, they fall faster and faster until they reach a speed of about 120 mph. At that speed, the upward force due to friction with the air becomes equal to the force of gravity pulling them downward.

You can see a similar effect if you release an egg in a tall jar of water. The egg soon reaches its terminal velocity as it falls. Try it and see!

But what will happen if the egg falls into a fluid in which it will float? Can you guess?

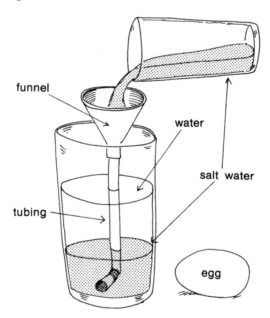

To test your prediction, prepare a saturated solution of salt in water—about 12 ounces (350 grams) per quart of water. Will an egg float in this solution? You can put a layer of salt water below some tap water in a tall jar using a funnel and tubing (see drawing) or a basting syringe. Pour the salt water slowly so that it disturbs the water above as little as possible. You might like to add food coloring to the solution so that you can easily distinguish it from the water.

What happens when you drop the egg into the layered liquids? Where else have you seen this effect?

UP OR DOWN

Materials: tall glass jar or bottle, eyedropper, water, rubber stopper or cork that fits mouth of bottle

Many things in the natural world fall and reach a terminal velocity—dust, leaves, raindrops, snowflakes, paper, and sky divers. Objects falling in water usually reach a terminal velocity very quickly, but there are some things, such as submarines, that can move either up or down. Here's a submarine that you can make for yourself.

Fill a jar with water. Leave about an inch or two for air at the top. Draw enough water into an eyedropper so that it floats in the jar with just the top of its rubber bulb above water.

Place the cork or stopper in the mouth of the jar. What happens to the eyedropper when you push down on the stopper? What happens when you release, lift, or remove the stopper from the jar? Can you make the "submarine" stay in the middle of the water so that it neither sinks nor floats? How do you explain the eyedropper's behavior when you push or pull on the stopper?

THE WAY THE BALL BOUNCES

Materials: different kinds of balls (tennis, golf, baseball, rubber, Ping-Pong, a marble, clay, superball, and so forth), yardstick, different surfaces (wood, concrete, tile, carpeting, newspaper, loose wood, and so forth), freezer, oven, tongs or large forceps or pot holders, an adult to help

---

Drop a ball from a height of 36 inches onto a hard floor. How high does it bounce? You'll have to get your head down beside the yardstick to see how high the bottom of the ball rises. Why should you always make your measurements from the bottom of the ball? Hint: How far does the ball actually fall and rise?

You will find the experiment a lot easier to do if you have someone help you. One person can drop the ball while the other watches to see how high it bounces.

What fraction of its original height does the ball attain on its first bounce? On its second bounce?

If you drop the ball from the height to which it rose on its first bounce, can you predict how high it will bounce this time? Can you predict how high it will bounce if you drop it from a height of 18 inches? From 12 inches?

Try dropping other kinds of balls onto the same surface. Which kind of ball is the bounciest? Which one is the least bouncy? (Did you try a ball of clay?) Which ball do you think will keep bouncing for the longest time?

Do you think the kind of surfaces the balls land on will have any effect on their bounce heights? To find out, try the same experiment on different surfaces such as concrete, tile, and carpeting. What do you find? Can you explain your results?

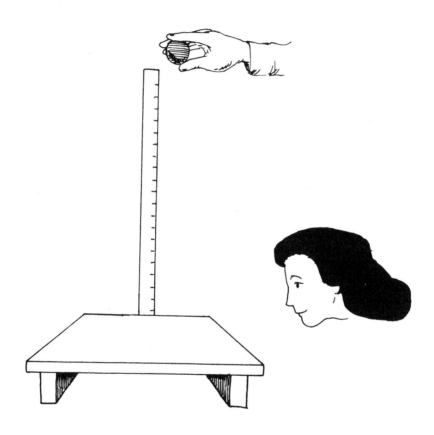

You may find it helpful, as you think about your results, to try dropping a ball on a firm wooden floor and then on a piece of wood balanced on two bricks or blocks as shown in the drawing.

71

To see if temperature has any effect on a ball's bounciness, first see how high the different balls bounce at room temperature. Then place the balls in a freezer (or outdoors if it is very cold) for about an hour. Remove the balls one at a time, and test their bounciness. Has the lower temperature changed the bounciness of any of the balls?

Can you predict what will happen to the bounciness of the balls if they are heated?

Ask an adult to help you test your predictions by placing the balls on a cookie pan and heating them in a warm (not hot) oven for a few minutes.

When the balls are warm use tongs, gloves, or a pot holder to remove them from the oven one at a time and test each ball for bounciness.

Are any of the balls bouncier than before? If they are, do they retian their bouncier nature after they cool?

If you haven't tried it yet, roll a piece of clay into a ball and drop it. Examine the clay carefully after it has fallen. Compare its shape with that of the other balls you dropped. Can you explain why the clay behaved differently?

What can you do to make a ball bounce higher than the height from which it is released? Is it easier to do this for some balls than for others? Are there any for which this is impossible?

FALLING SIDEWAYS

Materials: ruler, coins, bicycle, ball, balloon, water, chalk or stick

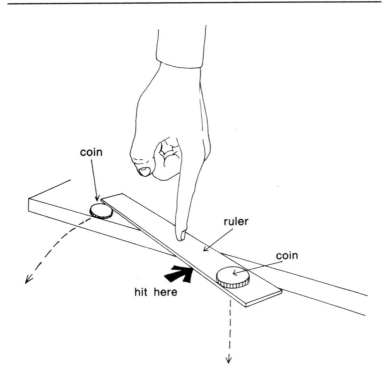

Galileo once asked what would happen if a sailor dropped a stone above the water from a high mast of a moving ship. Would the stone land at a point directly below where it was released, or would it

73

continue to move forward with the ship and land directly below the moving sailor?

He also wondered if the time it took the stone to fall would be different than if it were dropped without any horizontal motion.

You can find the answers to Galileo's questions by doing the following experiments.

- Place a coin on the edge of a table or counter. Place a second identical coin on the end of a ruler that projects out beyond the edge of the table. Put your index finger on the midpoint of the ruler; use your other hand to give the ruler a sharp hit toward the counter. The end of the ruler on the table should drive the coin at the table's edge horizontally outward. The other end of the ruler should move out from under the coin because the coin's inertia will make it stay put. Thus, one coin will fall straight down to the floor while the other one moves horizontally as it falls. Which coin do you think will strike the floor first? Or will both coins land at the same time?

  You can find the answer by listening carefully after you release the coins. Do you hear two distinct sounds as they land ·or just one?

- Draw a target on your sidewalk, path, or driveway with chalk or a stick. Ask a friend to ride a bike over the spot and drop a ball or a water balloon when he or she is directly above the target. Watch closely. Does the ball or balloon fall straight down and hit the target? Or does it continue to move with the bike and land beyond target?

  Now you get on your bike and try it. Where should you release the ball if you want to hit the target?

- Drop a bouncy ball as you walk over a hard floor. Do you have to stop to catch the ball as it bounces up or can you keep on walking and still catch it?

Try it again, but this time stop *immediately after* you release the ball. What happens to the ball?

- Watch the water coming from a hose that is held so the water emerges horizontally. If you could isolate a drop and let it fall from the nozzle of the hose, would it hit the ground before, after, or at the same time as a drop that was projected horizontally in the stream?

You can probably answer the last question based on what you've seen in earlier experiments. Can you also answer Galileo's questions?

On the moon the force of gravity is only one-sixth as strong as it is on earth. If you threw a ball on the moon, would it travel as far as it does on earth or would it travel farther?

A boy is standing on the rear platform of a train that is going 60 mph. At the instant he passes you, as you stand on a platform beside the tracks, he throws a ball straight back, away from the train. The boy can throw the ball at a speed of 60 mph. What path will you see the ball follow? What path will the ball follow as seen by the boy?

CHAPTER 5

PUSHES AND PULLS ALONG FLOORS AND COUNTERS

If you saw a book begin to slide along a table without being pushed, or a ball begin to bounce without having fallen, you might think poltergeists were at work. Certainly something unnatural would be happening. But why would you think so?

Sir Isaac Newton provided the answer more than three hundred years ago. He realized that objects move only when forces (pushes and pulls) are applied. He also noticed that when a force acts on an object, that object accelerates positively or negatively (speeds up or slows down). Sometimes accelerations are not easy to detect. You'll be able to understand acceleration better if you build an accelerometer. It will indicate the direction of the acceleration as well as its presence.

TWO KINDS OF ACCELEROMETERS

Materials: carpenter's level, tall pill bottle with cap, water, soap, half-pint jar with screw-on cap, cork, pin, thread, tape

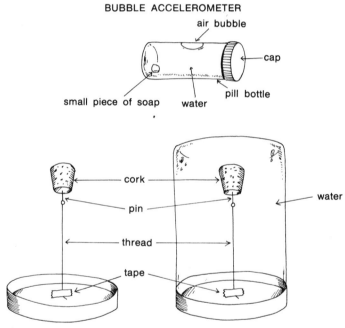

BUBBLE ACCELEROMETER

air bubble

cap

small piece of soap   water

pill bottle

cork

pin

water

thread

tape

CORK ACCELEROMETER

You can use a small carpenter's level as an accelerometer. Or you can build something similar by filling a tall thin pill bottle with water. Leave a little space at the top so there will be a bubble when you put the cap on. A tiny piece of soap in the bottle will prevent the bubble in your bubble accelerometer from sticking to the sides of the bottle.

To build a cork accelerometer, tie a piece of thread to the head of a straight pin. Stick the pin into a small cork or a piece of Styrofoam. Tape the free end of the thread to the center of the screw-on cap of a clear glass or plastic jar. Fill the jar brimful of water, screw on the cap, and invert the jar. Presto! you have an accelerometer.

Place an accelerometer on a countertop and move it gently back and forth. Watch what happens when you start or stop moving the accelerometer. Notice that the cork or bubble moves in the direction of the acceleration. The acceleration is always in the direction of the force—with the motion to start, against the motion to stop. Remember, to stop a body the force has to oppose the motion. The acceleration must be negative; that is, there must be a decrease in speed.

Take an accelerometer on a walk. Be sure to keep it level. Do you accelerate as you walk?

Take an accelerometer for an automobile ride. Can it detect accelerations in the car? Do any of the directions of acceleration surprise you?

BIG PULLS, LITTLE PULLS

Materials: accelerometer, fairly heavy toy truck or a small wagon, ruler, identical rubber bands or sensitive spring scale

---

Mount an accelerometer on a toy truck or a small wagon. Attach a rubber band or a spring scale to the front of the truck or wagon. How big a stretch is needed to make the vehicle move along with a slow but constant speed? This is the minimum force needed to overcome friction. (You can measure the stretch on a rubber band by placing it above a ruler as you pull it.)

Pull the toy again. This time stretch the rubber band more than enough to overcome friction. Keep the rubber band stretched the same amount as you pull. What happens to the truck or wagon's speed as you pull? What does your accelerometer indicate?

Repeat the experiment, but double the force by stretching *two* side-by-side rubber bands as much as you stretched one before. What happens to the acceleration as the force gets bigger?

FORCE, MATTER, AND MORE MATTER

Materials: same as previous experiment and some weights to add to the truck or wagon

What do you think will happen to the acceleration of your truck or wagon if you add more weight to it without changing the force?

Test your prediction by first accelerating the vehicle with a certain force. Then add weight so that the amount of matter is at least doubled. Repeat the experiment using the same force. What happens to the acceleration of the truck? Were you right?

MAKING THINGS GO ROUND AND ROUND

Materials: accelerometer, clear tape, record player turntable or lazy Susan, marking pen, cardboard

You probably weren't surprised to find that heavy things move more sluggishly than lighter ones given the same force. Nor were you startled to learn that bigger forces give bigger accelerations. After all, you know that you can accelerate a tennis ball a lot more easily than a bowling ball, and that a tennis ball will attain a greater speed if you hit it harder.

The interesting thing is that Newton used this simple understanding of force and acceleration to explain the movement of the planets and stars as well as that of falling bodies and horse-drawn carriages. In fact, he used it to explain all motion.

But planets move about the sun in circles (almost) with nearly constant speed. Can a force be acting on them if they are moving at constant speed?

You can do a simple experiment to find out. Hold an accelerometer at arm's length (be sure it is level) and turn about watching the accelerometer as you turn.

What do you find?

To see what's hapening in more detail, tape an accelerometer to a turntable or lazy Susan. When the table turns at a steady speed is there an acceleration?

Were you surprised? What was the direction of the acceleration? What must have been the direction of the force?

To see if the acceleration is related to the speed, change the speed of the turntable, or move the accelerometer closer to and then farther from the center of the spinning table. Where is the speed of a spinning table greatest? Where is its speed zero?

How is the acceleration affected by the speed?

See if you can predict the direction of the acceleration on a playground merry-go-round, a toy train moving along a circular track, or a car rounding a curve.

By the way, have you ever tried to draw a straight line on a spinning turntable.

Cut a piece of cardboard to fit the turntable and fasten it on with tape.

Can you figure out a way to draw a circle on a spinning table? It's really very easy. But try to draw a straight line from the center to the edge of the table while it is turning.

Not so easy, is it? Can you figure out a way to do it? *Hint;* How does the speed of any point on the table change as you move outward from the center?

AN INWARD FORCE

Materials: plastic pail, water

Newton knew that an inward acceleration indicated an inward force. He also realized that a force was needed to change the *direction* of a circling body's motion. After all, a change in direction is as important as a change in speed.

The inward force causing something to move in a circle is called a centripetal force. You can feel such a force by doing the following experiment.

Fill a plastic pail about one-fourth full of water. Take it outdoors or someplace where you can swing it without hitting anything or having to worry about spilling.

Swing the pail in a *vertical* circle that extends from over your head to very near the ground. (Don't worry, the water will stay in the pail.) You'll feel the force your arm exerts to keep the pail moving in a circle.

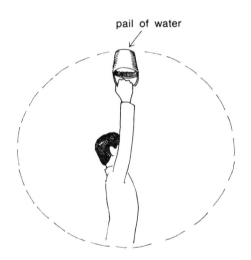

pail of water

From what you already know about acceleration in circular motion, would you expect the required force to increase or decrease if you swing the pail faster? Were you right?

If you add more water to the pail, will the force needed for circular motion at the same speed be greater, less, or the same? Try it!

Why do you think water stays in the pail even while it is upside down? *Hint:* Suppose the centripetal acceleration of the pail is greater than the acceleration due to gravity.

Perhaps you've gone through a loop-the-loop on a roller coaster. If you have, then you know what it's like to be the water in the pail.

THE PUSH/PUSH BACK LAW

Materials: two toy trucks or cars, spring-type clothespin, tape, weights, rubber band

When you swing a pail in a circle, you have to pull it inward to constantly change its direction. But you can feel the pail pulling outward on your arm. If you and a friend are on roller or ice skates and you give your friend a push, he or she will move away from you. At the same time, you too will move, but in the opposite direction.

Again, it was Newton who first realized that forces always come in pairs. If you push on something living or nonliving, that thing pushes back on you with an equal force in the opposite direction.

This is Newton's third law of motion, but we'll call it the "push/push back law."

To see this law in action, without being directly involved in the pushing, try this experiment. Find two toy cars or trucks that are reasonably large. Tape a spring-type clothespin upside down to one of the trucks or cars. Push the vehicles together to compress the spring. Release both cars at the same time. Does Newton's law seem to apply?

What do you think will happen if you repeat the experiment after adding some weight to one of the trucks? Try it! Which truck moved faster? Does it make any difference which truck is heavier?

Replace one truck with something much heavier. Stretch the spring by pushing the truck against a wall. Now the pushes are between the truck and the earth. (After all, the wall is part of the house, which is firmly attached to the earth.) What do you find when you release the truck? What do you think will happen to the truck's speed after release if you add weight to the truck?

Try to predict what will happen if you give the truck with the clothespin attached, and open, a push so that it collides with the other identical truck. How will the push given by the moving truck affect the stationary truck? How will the push given to the moving truck by the one at rest change its motion? Remember, Newton said the pushes will be equal but opposite in direction.

What happens if one truck is heavier than the other? Does it matter whether the moving or stationary truck is heavier? What happens if the truck collides with the wall (earth)?

From what you have learned about collisions, how do you think cars and highways might be designed in order to make them safer?

When you walk or run, you get your push *forward* by pushing your feet *backward* against the earth. Does your push on the earth make it move? What happens when you try to step from an untied rowboat onto a dock? When you try to walk on very slippery ice? When you walk in loose sand?

Do you think Newton's law applies to pulls as well as pushes? To find out, connect your two trucks with a stretched rubber band so they pull on each other when you release them. Repeat the experiments you did using pulls instead of pushes. Are the results similar?

A ROCKET BOAT

Materials: water, sink or bathtub, long balloon, milk carton

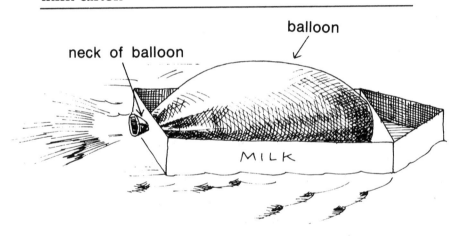

A rocket is an example of the push/push back law. You can make a "rocket" boat as shown in the drawing. Make the hole in the back of the boat, through which you pull the mouth of the balloon, small enough so that the "fuel" will last for several seconds. What happens when you release the rocket? Why is the rocket an example of Newton's law?

86

FRICTION: SOMETHING THAT'S ALWAYS WITH US

Materials: washers, thread, smooth board, wooden blocks, paper clips, sandpaper, aluminum foil, waxed paper, thumb tacks, rubber bands, newspaper, toy car

---

In your experiments you've kept frictional forces small by using cars on wheels, marbles, and motions in air. But in most normal activities friction plays an important, often vital, part. Imagine what it would be like to try to walk without friction between your feet and the floor or ground. Or of how useless cars, buses, and trains would be without friction.

Galileo and Newton were able to understand motion better than others because they could understand what motion would be like *without* friction. But they both knew that friction was a force that always acted against motion. You saw what frictionless motion is like by building an air car (Chapter 4).

Friction is always present when one surface moves over another. But you've probably noticed that frictional forces vary with different kinds of surfaces. For example, it is much easier to walk over a rubber mat than over a polished floor or an icy side-walk.

You can use a simple friction tester shown in the next drawing to measure the friction between surfaces. Place a smooth block on the board and add washers to the hook until the block slides with a steady speed. The number of washers required to move the block is a measure of the friction opposing the motion.

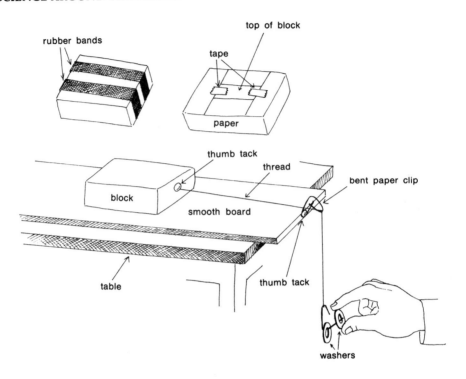

Does it take more washers to make the block begin to move than it does to keep it moving once started?

If you find starting friction is greater than the friction once the block is in motion, try tapping the board as you add washers to free the block.

Is friction related to weight? To find out, put a second, identical block on the first one. Or add weights equal to the weight of the block. Is the friction greater? Is it twice as great?

Does the area of the surfaces rubbing together affect friction? If the block is smooth on all sides, turn it so it rests on a narrower side and see if it changes the number of washers you must add to make the block slide. If the block is not as smooth on its narrow side, cover it with a smooth material—aluminum foil or newspaper, for instance—then test the effect of changing the area. What do you find?

Tape a sheet of sandpaper to the block. How many washers are needed to make the block slide now?

Repeat the experiment but cover the bottom of the block with aluminum foil, newspaper, waxed paper, or construction paper. You can put wide rubber bands around the block to make a rubber surface. You can also change the surface of the board by taping various things such as aluminum foil to it. You can test to see the effect of putting the block on rollers (round pencils work well). Try a variety of surfaces and keep a record of your results. What pair of surfaces provide the most friction? The least?

Another way to test friction is to raise the board as you tap it. Raise one end of the board until the block slides. Then measure the height you lifted the board or the angle it makes with the tabletop. Do your results on this test agree with those of your earlier experiment?

CHAPTER **6**

SCIENCE
ON THE
CEILING

In Chapter 5 you saw that the push/push back law can explain why a rocket boat moves. The same law can explain the motion of all rocket-driven vehicles: jet planes, jet-propelled cars, and the rockets used to launch satellites and the space shuttle. In air and in the vast emptiness of space above the atmosphere the resistance to motion is less than in water. That is why rocket-propelled vehicles move so much faster in air and space than in water. To see that this is true, make your own balloon-propelled air rocket.

A BALLOON ROCKET

Materials: long balloon, thread, soda straw, tie band, clear tape

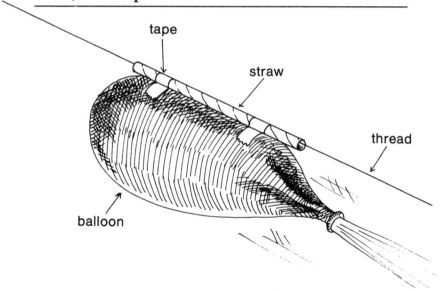

Blow up a balloon and let it go. Can you explain its motion? To see the motion more clearly you can make the "rocket" follow a straight-line path. Set up the rocket as shown in the drawing. Attach the balloon to the soda straw with clear tape. (You can seal the balloon with a tie band while you attach it.)

Release the balloon and watch it get smaller as it pushes air out the back. Do you have any evidence that the air pushed on the balloon? Did the balloon rocket move faster than the boat?

A CIRCLING SATELLITE

Materials: clear cake cover or round clear baking dish, marble or golf ball

---

Rockets are used to send satellites and space shuttles into orbit about the earth. Once they are in orbit, gravity provides the centripetal force required to maintain the motion. But what would happen if there were no force on the satellite?

To find out, place a marble or a golf ball under a clear circular dish or cake cover. By moving the dish quickly in small circles, you can make the marble move swiftly along the circumference of the dish. Where will the marble go if you suddenly lift one side of the dish?

Which of the paths in the drawing best describes the route taken by the marble?

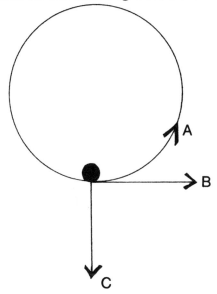

WHAT KEEPS AN AIRPLANE UP?

Materials: Ping-pong ball, mailing tube or newspaper, drinking glass, balloons, thread, soda straws, paper, tape, paper clips, funnel, vacuum cleaner

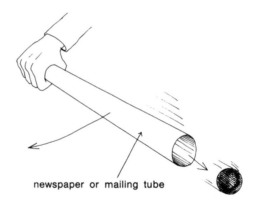

newspaper or mailing tube

Satellites and space shuttles can travel through the thin air of the upper atmosphere and even through the vastness of empty space because the principle of push/push back enables them to maneuver anywhere as long as they have fuel to push against. Even jet planes can travel in very thin air, but propeller-driven planes and gliders can fly only in the denser air near earth's surface.

How does an airplane or a glider get the lift it needs to stay aloft? You may be surprised to find that it's the result of the same forces that make a baseball curve.

You can throw a Ping-Pong curve ball every time if you launch it from a mailing tube or a newspaper rolled into a cone. Flip the ball from the tube or cone by swinging the tube from left to right with a snap of your wrist as you bring your right arm across your body. (See the drawing.) Which way does the ball curve? Which way does the ball curve if you launch it with your left hand swinging the tube from right to left?

As you swing the tube, the ball is made to spin as it rolls along its "launchpad." Which way is the ball spinning when you swing the tube from left to right? From right to left?

When a spinning ball moves through air, it drags air along with it on one side; on the other side it is turning against the air and so resists the air flow. Thus, air flows by the ball faster on one side than the other.

The experiments below will help you to understand what effect the difference in air flow has on the ball.

- Hold one soda straw upright in a glass of water. Use a second straw to blow an air stream over the top of the first

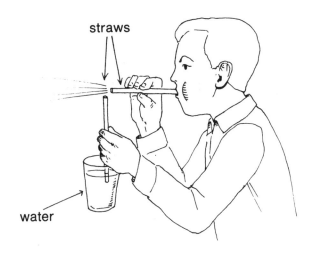

straws

water

straw. What happens to the pressure above the water in the vertical straw? How can you tell? (Remember, when you started, the pressure on the water inside and outside the straw was equal; both water levels were the same.) Can you blow hard enough to make the straws behave like an atomizer in a spray can or a perfume bottle?

- Hang two balloons several inches apart. From the previous experiment can you predict what will happen if you blow between the balloons? Try it! Which presses harder against the balloons, the moving air between them or the still air on their other sides?

What will happen if you blow on the side of just one of these balloons?

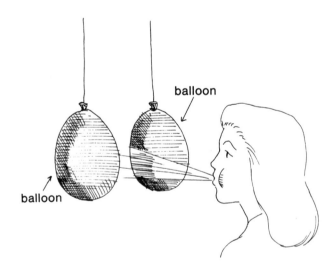

balloon

balloon

The faster a stream of fluid moves, the less it pushes to the sides. This fact was discovered by a Swiss scientist named

Daniel Bernoulli in the eighteenth century. It was nearly two centuries before his discovery was used to lift heavier-than-air craft.

- From what you've learned, see if you can explain why you can't blow a Ping-Pong ball out of an upright funnel as shown in the drawing.

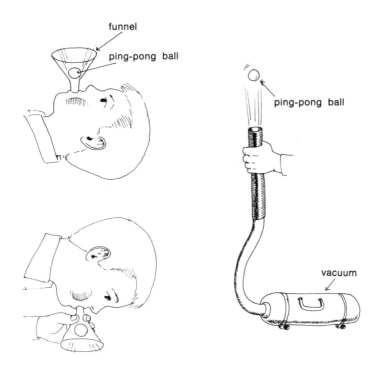

funnel

ping-pong ball

ping-pong ball

vacuum

Why will it remain in the tube, instead of falling, if you blow down into the funnel as shown in the next drawing? (You can support the ball and then let go after you start blowing.)

97

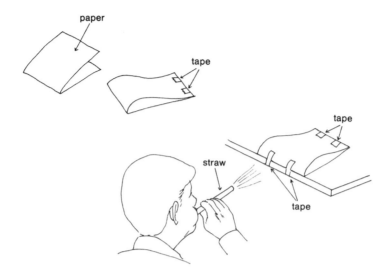

- If you have a vacuum cleaner that will blow as well as suck air, you can make a Ping-Pong ball "float" in a stream of air as shown in the drawing.
- Now let's look at some experiments that show more directly how Bernoulli's principle is related to the lift on an airplane or glider.

   Cut a piece of paper about 3 by 7 inches. Fold the paper so that one side is a little longer than the other. With the longer piece over the shorter one, tape the ends together so that the top is curved, as in the drawing. Tape this section of an "airplane wing" to the edge of a counter or table. Blow gently against the front edge of the wing with a soda straw. What happens? Now try blowing harder.

   Air passing over an airplane wing reaches the back edge of the wing at the same time as does the air flowing under the wing. Because the distance over the curved upper side of the wing is greater than the distance along the flatter underside, air moving over the wing moves faster than the air that flows underneath. What effect will this have on the wing?

Will a wing with more curvature on the upper side provide more lift than one that is less curved? Design an experiment to find out!

PAPER GLIDERS

Materials: paper, paper clips, tape

Here is one design for making a paper glider from a single sheet of paper. Make one and test it to see how well it flies.

Now design one of your own to see if you can make a glider that flies farther and straighter. You might even sponsor a contest among your friends to see who can make the best glider from a single sheet of paper.

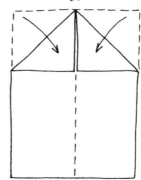

1. Fold a piece of paper in half the long way.

2. Open the sheet. Fold the corners to the center to make a triangle.

3.

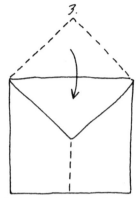

Fold the triangle back
onto the square.

4.

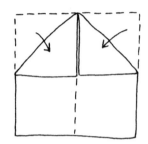

Fold the new corner of the
square back to the center
to make another triangle.
Now fold along the center
dotted line . . .

5.

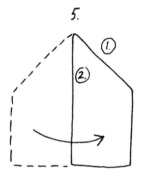

. . . to bring the two halves
together. Now fold edge 1
down onto edge 2 . . .

6.

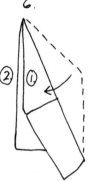

. . . on each side to form
a pair of "wings" (when
released) and a single
"fuselage."

100

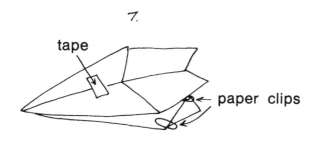

7.

tape

paper clips

Fold up the wings and use a little tape to hold them together. You may want to add a paper clip or two to improve the "ship's" glide pattern.

OTHER WAYS TO REACH THE CEILING

Materials: Ping-Pong ball, sink or bathtub, helium-filled balloon, string or yarn, balloons, electromagnet (iron nail, enameled wire, batteries, tape), paper clips, sandpaper

You saw in Chapter 2 that a solid weighs less in a liquid than it does in air. You also found that air appears to weigh nothing in air. In fact, any object in a fluid (a gas or liquid) is buoyed (lifted) by a force equal to the weight of the fluid it displaces.

- If you push a Ping-Pong ball under the surface of some water in a sink or bathtub, you can feel the buoyant force. What happens when you release the ball well below the surface of the water?
- If you can obtain a helium balloon, attach a long piece of string or yarn to the neck of the balloon. How long a piece of string can the balloon lift? If it rises all the way to the ceiling, you may have to add a paper clip or two to the string.

  Carefully release a little helium from the balloon. What do you predict about the length of string that the helium balloon will be able to lift now? Were you right?

  See if you can adjust the length of string so that the balloon neither rises nor sinks. At this point, how does the

101

weight of balloon and string compare with the weight of the air displaced?

If you leave a balloon for a few hours, helium will leak out of it. How can you tell?

Why can't you make a balloon filled with carbon dioxide float in air? Is there any way to make an air-filled balloon float in air?

- Of course, you can use a magnet to lift things, but did you know that you can use electricity to lift things? Wrap some enamel-coated (insulated) wire around a 3- or 4-inch iron nail. Wrap the wire in the same direction (clockwise or counter-clockwise) all along the length of the nail until it is two or three layers thick.

Sandpaper the ends of the wire to remove the insulation. Leave about a foot of wire free at each end. Use a little tape to hold the wrapped wire in place. Connect the free ends of the wire to opposite ends of a D-cell battery and you have an electromagnet.

Try using your electromagnet to lift metal objects such as paper clips. *Don't leave the electromagnet connected to the battery for very long.* If you do, your battery will wear out quickly.

What kinds of things will the electromagnet lift? What kinds of things won't it lift?

- If it's wintertime, you can use static electricity to hold balloons on the ceiling or against walls. Just rub a balloon briskly on your clothing and "stick" it on the wall or ceiling. (This experiment probably won't work in summer months; there is generally too much moisture in the air.)

- Just for fun, while you have a charge on one of the balloons, hold it near a thin stream of water coming from a faucet. What happens to the stream? Why do you think this happens?

CHAPTER 7

LIGHT UP YOUR LIFE

Most of the light we see comes from the sun and enters our homes through windows. Trees, grass, and flowers are visible only because they reflect sunlight to our eyes. Even moonlight is sunlight reflected from the moon's surface. At night, we use light produced by electricity, but, regardless of its source, light behaves in the same way.

REFLECTED LIGHT

Materials: plane mirror

Hold a plane (flat) mirror in a beam of sunlight coming through a window. Use the mirror to reflect a patch of bright light around the room. Are there any places to which you cannot reflect the light? Is the angle at which the light strikes the mirror related to the position of the light patch on the wall or ceiling?

IMAGES IN A PLANE MIRROR

Materials: plane mirror, paper, yardstick, ruler, pins, scissors, cardboard, finishing nail, clay, protractor, light source, construction paper or 5-by-8-inch index card

---

Look directly into a mirror to see your image. If you hold your hand between part of your face and the mirror, that part of your image will not be seen. Why does part of your image disappear?

Wink your right eye; which eye does your image wink? Hold up your right hand; which hand does your image raise?

Ask a friend to stand to one side of a mirror while you stand on the other side. Stand far enough to the side so that you cannot see your own image. Can you see the image of your friend? If you can see your friend's image, can he or she see your image? When you stand so that you can't see your friend's image, can he or she see yours? Is the path followed by reflected light reversible?

As you move closer to a mirror, do you see more or less of the background behind you reflected in the mirror? Can you explain why?

If you stand in front of a mirror one foot long, what length of your own body do you see reflected by the mirror? To find out, measure the height of a mirror with a yardstick. Now stand away from the mirror and hold the yardstick vertically right beside one eye. How

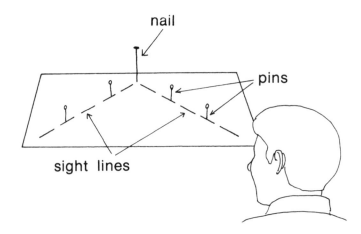

much of the yardstick do you see reflected? Move farther from and then closer to the mirror and repeat your experiment. How much of the yardstick do you see reflected by the mirror in each of these positions? Would you really need a full-length mirror in order to see your entire body reflected in a mirror? Do you think it's an accident that at the position of your eye you can see a length that is always exactly twice the height of the mirror?

Where does the reflected image of an object appear to be? Is it on, behind, or in front of the mirror? To find out, you can use sight lines to locate the image. Before you do that, you might like to practice drawing sight lines to something that you can see more directly.

Place a piece of paper on a sheet of cardboard. Push a finishing nail through the center of the paper into the cardboard. Take a pair of pins, stand back away from the nail, and use the pins to establish a straight line (a sight line) from your eye to the nail, as in the drawing. Make other sight lines to the nail from other positions using a different pair of pins each time. Use a ruler to draw the straight lines made by each pair of pins. It should come as no surprise that the lines meet at the nail.

105

Put the finishing nail a couple of inches in front of a mirror as shown in the drawing. Use pins to make several sight lines to the image of the nail seen in the mirror. Where will these sight lines meet?

Draw a line on the paper along the rear edge of the mirror. Then move the mirror and use a ruler to draw the sight lines. Where do they meet? What does this tell you? How do the distances of the image and the nail from the mirror compare? Repeat the experiment with the nail closer to and farther from the mirror. Are nail and image always equal in distance from the mirror?

How did the light that gave rise to the image get from the nail to a sight line to your eye? Draw the path that one narrow beam of light (a light ray) must have followed. How does the angle that the reflected ray makes with the mirror's surface compare with the one made by the ray from the nail and the mirror?

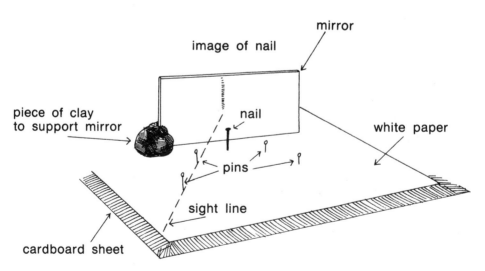

mirror

image of nail

piece of clay
to support mirror

nail

white paper

pins

sight line

cardboard sheet

106

To see more clearly how the angles made by light striking and reflecting from a mirror compare, try this experiment. Cut a thin, vertical slit, about $1/16$ inch wide, in the center of a 5-by-8-inch index card or a piece of construction paper of similar size. Fold the sides of the paper so the "ray maker" will stand by itself, and place it on a table or counter several feet from a strong light source as shown in the drawing.

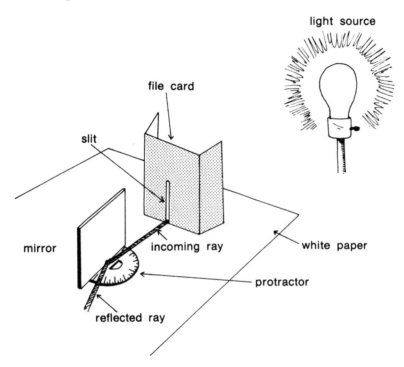

Place a sheet of white paper behind the ray maker so that you can see the ray clearly. Now place your mirror on the beam and see how it reflects light as you turn the mirror to change the angle at which the light ray strikes the mirror. As you make the angle between the

107

mirror and the incoming ray bigger, what happens to the angle between the mirror and the reflected ray?

Use a protractor to measure the angles between the incoming ray and the mirror and the reflected ray and the mirror. Measure a variety of angles. What do you find about the two angles?

To see how images appear to form behind mirrors, place a light quite close to your ray maker as shown in the drawing below. Notice how the reflected beam seems to be coming from a point behind the mirror just as an image does.

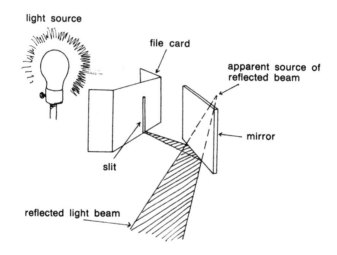

MULTI-MIRRORS

Materials: two plane mirrors, pin or nail or other small object, light source, ray maker, white paper, pencil

---

What do you think you'll see if you look into two mirrors that are at right angles to each other? Before predicting, you might like to use your ray maker to see what happens to a ray of light that strikes one of the mirrors. Place a pin, nail, or similar small object between the mirrors. Why do you think there are three images?

Now put your face between the mirrors. Look at the image where the mirrors meet. (If the mirrors are at right angles, the image between the mirrors will be complete and not distorted.)

Wink your right eye. Which eye does the image in the right mirror wink? How about the one in the left mirror? Which eye does the middle image wink? How do you explain these results?

Put the mirrors together so that one is vertical and the other horizontal. Put your face between the mirrors again. What do you notice about the middle image this time?

Put your head or a small object between the two mirrors and slowly decrease the angle between the mirrors. What happens to the number of images you see as the angle grows smaller?

Hold two mirrors parallel to each other. Place a pencil between the mirrors. How many images do you see?

MIRROR WRITING

Materials: Mirror, paper, pencil

Place a plane mirror perpendicular to the print on this page. Look at the reflected print in the mirror. Is the image of the print upside down? Is it reversed left for right?

Leonardo da Vinci wrote all his notes so they had to be read in a mirror. See if you can write your name so that it can be read with a mirror.

109

Look at the figures in the drawing. Can you change the rectangle into a square by placing your mirror on it? Can you make a circle from the semicircle? Can you make a hexagon? A diamond? Can you fix the broken cylinder?

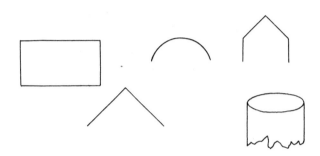

IMAGES FROM A PINHOLE

Materials: candle and candle holder or light bulb, 5-by-8-inch index card or piece of heavy paper, pin or sharp instrument, ruler or yardstick, light-colored wall or light screen (white paper taped to cardboard), an adult to help

Ask an adult to help you with this experiment if you use a candle flame as a light source. You can use an ordinary light bulb, but a candle flame is prettier.

Place a light source near a wall or light screen in a dark room. Use a pin to make a small hole in a card or sheet of heavy paper. Hold the card between the light and the screen or wall. You should be able to see an image of the light source on the screen. Is the image upside down or right side up? Can you explain how the image is formed? What happens as you change the distance between screen and pinhole? Between light and pinhole?

What happens to the image when you make the pinhole bigger? Smaller?

What happens if you make a second pinhole? A third? Many?

On a clear day you can make images of the sun with a pinhole. Remember, it's safe to look at the image of the sun on a screen but *don't look directly at the sun.*

BENDING LIGHT

Materials: drinking glass or jar, water, sharp scissors, paper, 5-by-8-inch index card or heavy paper, pencil, light bulb

It's true that light usually travels in straight lines, but when it goes from one substance to another at an angle, it bends. To see this, put a pencil in a glass of water. Look at it from the side. See how the pencil appears to be broken at the point where it enters the water.

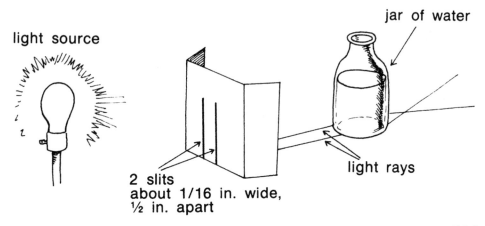

light source

jar of water

2 slits
about 1/16 in. wide,
½ in. apart

light rays

111

If you place the same glass of water on a sheet of paper in a beam of sunlight or near a light bulb, you can see that the cylinder of water brings light together. Hold a white card near the "water-jar lens" and you can see that the lens pulls the light together to form a sharp, bright line of light.

The bending of light is called refraction. To see more directly how it works, prepare a new ray maker as shown in the drawing and place a jar or glass of water on the rays to see how they are brought together.

BENDING LIGHT WITH A LENS

Materials: convex lens (magnifying glass), light screen of white paper taped to cardboard, clay, ruler, candle and holder or light bulb, eyedropper, paper clip, glossy page with print

You find lenses in many places: eyeglasses, telescopes, microscopes, binoculars, magnifiers, and so forth. There are two kinds of lenses: convex, which bow outward like a ball, and concave, which bow inward like a dish. Magnifying glasses are convex lenses. They are quite common, so you can probably find one to experiment with.

A convex lens has a principal focus—a point where parallel rays of light are brought together. To find this point, hold a convex lens in a beam of sunlight. Bring a light screen toward the side of the lens away from the sun. Look for the sharpest point of light that the lens will form; that point is the principal focus. Measure the distance from the lens to the principal focus; it is called the focal length of the lens. What is the focal length of your lens?

If you hold your lens close to some print, you can see that it magnifies. But what happens as you move the lens more than a focal length away from the print?

A lens will form real images; that is, images you can see or "capture" on a screen. To see such an image, stand away from a window and hold a light screen about a focal length behind your lens. You should be able to find some clear images on the screen.

To investigate the images formed by a convex lens, use some clay to hold your lens several focal lengths away from a burning candle or small light bulb in a dark room. If you use a candle, be sure an adult is available to help you. With a light screen, locate the image of the flame or light bulb. Is the image right side up or inverted?

What happens to the size of the image and the distance from lens to image as you move the light closer to the principal focus? As you move the light farther from the principal focus?

If you have two convex lenses, try to make a simple microscope by holding them one above the other over some print. Try to make a telescope.

To make a primitive magnifier, use an eyedropper to place a small drop of water on some print on a glossy page in a magazine. Or, if you want to be a bit fancier, bend a paper clip to make a small loop at one end and a handle at the other. Place a drop of water on the loop and you have a miniature microscope. Use it to examine some colored print in a magazine. You will see that the color actually consists of many tiny dots.

RAINBOWS IN THE ROOM

Materials: plane mirror, pan, water, light screen

You have seen that water bends light. Now you'll see that some colors are bent more than others. The result is a rainbow, or spectrum, of colors.

113

Place a mirror in a pan of water so that one end is submerged, as in the drawing. Place the pan in a beam of sunlight so that light reflects from the submerged mirror. Move a light screen around until you "capture" the rainbow. (You may find the spectrum on a wall or the ceiling.) What colors are combined in ordinary white light?

There will also be a bright patch of white light. How can you show that this light is reflected from the end of the mirror that is *not* under water?

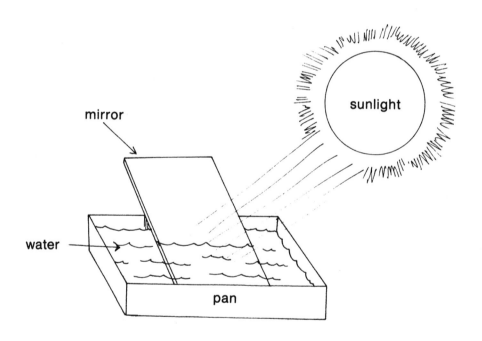

SHADOWS

**Materials: several frosted light bulbs, light bulb
with a straight filament or a box with a small hole,
large coin or disk, fluorescent light and other light
sources, large sheet of paper, scissors, light screen,
mirror, pencil**

Turn on a frosted bulb at one end of an otherwise dark room. Use your hand to cast a shadow on the opposite wall. Move your hand toward and then away from the light. What happens to the size of the shadow? When is the shadow most distinct? When is it fuzziest?

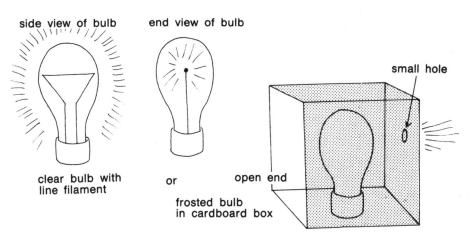

side view of bulb   end view of bulb

clear bulb with
line filament

or   open end

frosted bulb
in cardboard box

small hole

115

Why does the size of your shadow change here but not in a beam of sunlight?

If you can find a clear bulb with a straight filament, you can turn it so it looks like a point of light. If you can't, make a point source of light by punching a ½-inch hole in a box that you place in front of a large frosted bulb. Be sure that the bulb does not touch the box and that the box is open so heat can escape. Because little light comes through the hole, you may have to move it closer to a wall.

Compare the shadows made with a frosted bulb and a point source of light. How do they differ? Why do you think they are different?

Place a frosted bulb about 2 feet from a wall. Use a large coin or similar disk to cast a shadow on the wall. You should be able to find a dark shadow (the umbra) inside a lighter shadow called the penumbra. How can you change the size of the umbra? Can you make the umbra disappear?

To explain why there is an umbra and a penumbra, close one eye and hold the disk in front of your other eye while you look at the frosted bulb. Where can you hold the disk so no light from the bulb enters your eye? How should you place the disk so that you can see light from the edges of the bulb? Now can you explain why some parts of the shadow are darker than others? Look in the encyclopedia to find out about eclipses of the sun. How is this experiment related to eclipses?

Can you find a way to make two shadows of your hand? How can you make one of the shadows darker than the other? Bigger than the other? Can you make three shadows of your hand? Many?

How can you make colored shadows? Look around a lighted Christmas tree or other colored lights for ideas on how to do this.

You've seen the shadows made by a point of light and a frosted bulb. See if you can predict what the shadows will be like if made by a candle, a flashlight, a spotlight, a fluorescent light, or the sun.

116

Watch the shadow of a pencil as you turn it near a wall illuminated by a fluorescent bulb. Why does the shadow change so much?

Can you reflect a shadow? Use a light, a pencil, and a mirror to find out.

Make a profile cutout of a friend by using a point source of light to cast his or her shadow on a large sheet of paper. Draw the outline of the shadow. Then cut it out with scissors. How can you make the profile larger? Smaller? Can the shadow profile ever be smaller than the person's profile?

INDEX

ABOUT
THE AUTHOR

ROBERT GARDNER is head of the science department at Salisbury School, Salisbury, Connecticut, where he teaches physics, chemistry, and physical science. He did his undergraduate work at Wesleyan University and has graduate degrees from Trinity College and Wesleyan University. He has taught in a number of National Science Foundation teachers' institutes and is the author of several science books, including *Kitchen Chemistry; Water, The Life Sustaining Resource;* and *The Whale Watchers' Guide.*